Copyright © 2016 Brad Bordessa

First Printing, 2016

ISBN: 978-1533350398

Visit my website at: liveukulele.com

Table of Contents

Mahalo

For my 'ukulele 'ohana across the globe. Thank you for the support.

~ ~

Thanks especially to Chuck Moore for creating the beautiful instrument I use to explore the world of music.

To Jo Kim for reminding me to keep it simple.

And to James Hill for inspiration, encouragement, and advice.

~ ~

Glenn Reither, Daniel Newton, Jody Mace, Kris Bordessa, and Herb Ohta, Jr. all provided feedback on the material. A second pair of eyeballs is priceless.

~ ~

The biggest thank you, of course, is to YOU for bringing this book into your life! May 'Ukulele Chord Shapes serve you well on your musical journey.

Introduction

There are quite a few 'ukulele chord books floating around that show you one chord per box (here's a C, here's a D, etc...). These are static shapes - great for getting a quick start, but single-use only. That's a shame because with a little added information you can take each of those shapes and play 11 more chords. Sound appealing? Welcome to the world of *'Ukulele Chord Shapes*.

This is a do-it-yourself book. If you need to learn how to play Cm7, F9, and Bbmaj7 for *Autumn Leaves* **right now**, this book is probably going to leave you in a bind. You won't find many static solutions here. What you will find is a variable-based approach and tools for understanding the 'ukulele better.

On the following pages you will find charts that show a highlighted root note telling you where to play a chord; information on building chords; and many tidbits.

In order to get the most out of the information here, you have to be patient and work your way through the pages, experimenting as you go. The shapes method has a bit of a learning curve and will take some time to fully sink in, but in the long run I believe it will give you a more comprehensive view of the fretboard and how chords work together to form songs.

Baritone, English, and Other Tunings

Rejoice! This book works with any 'ukulele tuned in intervals of a 4th, a 3rd, and a 4th. This includes (but is not limited to):

- Standard **G C E A**
- Baritone **D G B E**
- English **A D F# B**

The shapes found in this book will work with each as long as you have the correct fretboard chart for your instrument (several of which can be found in the final pages). That said, all examples are for G C E A tuned 'ukuleles, but just do some mental transposing to your tuning of choice and follow along.

1

How To Use This Book

Instead of using one-off chord diagrams, this book shows *shapes* for each chord type. The diagrams show the location of the root inside each voicing so you can see which fret to start the shape from. In this manner you can use every shape in all 12 keys.

What follows is an in-depth walk-through of how this method works.

Along the way you will see glossary terms highlighted in ***bold italics***. An explanation of each can be found on page 54.

THE FRETBOARD

Below is a ***fingerboard*** chart (also called the fretboard). It is the foundation of this book. *"Mr. Fingerboard, this is Mr. 'Ukulele Player. Shake hands…"*

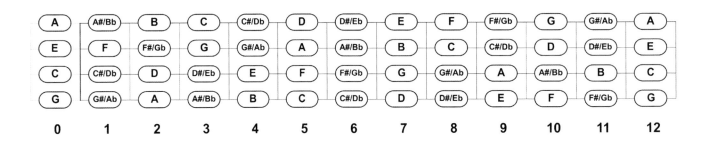

If you know the location of all the notes already – great! If not, you'd better learn them!

Fretboard Diagram Orientation:

The G, 4th-string (bottom horizontal line) is the top string and closest to your face as you hold the 'ukulele. The A, 1st-string (top horizontal line) is the bottom string and closest to the floor.

Take some time to get familiar with where the notes live. You don't need to have the whole fretboard memorized to move on to the charts, but do yourself a favor and learn where each note is on every string. It will be *very* useful in many more applications than just here.

If you're using other tunings, or just want a dedicated refrence to look at, there are a collection of fretboard maps in the back of the book.

FRETBOARD MEMORIZATION TIPS:

- Learn the open strings first. It's obvious, but you need to know them *really* well.

- The 12th fret is the same as the open strings. Any higher and all the notes repeat.

- The ***natural notes*** are easiest to remember. Start with those.

- The 5th and 7th frets host only natural notes. (And they usually have marker dots!)

- The C scale is made up of natural notes. Kill two birds with one stone and learn it!

- Once you have the natural notes down, work on the sharps and flats in between.

CHORD DIAGRAMS

A *chord diagram* (or chord "box") is a line representation of the 'ukulele's fretboard showing which frets and strings your fingers go on to form a chord.

A grid makes up 75% of a chord diagram. Vertical lines represent the strings **(Fig. 1)**, with the G string on the left and the A string on the right. The horizontal lines are frets **(Fig. 2)**. The chord box can show as many frets as necessary (four is standard, but I've seen as many as 12).

When the diagram starts at the nut, the top "fret" line is usually thicker to represent the end of the fretboard. If the box starts midway up the neck, the starting fret will be marked with a number to the side and the nut line will no longer be emphasized.

The last part of a chord diagram are the finger dots **(Fig. 3)**. They are located on the string lines and between the fret lines to show where your fingers are placed for each chord.

In some chord diagrams you might see a hollow dot at the top of the box above one or more of the string lines. This means to play the open string without a fretted finger. An "X" in the same location means the string is not played at all.

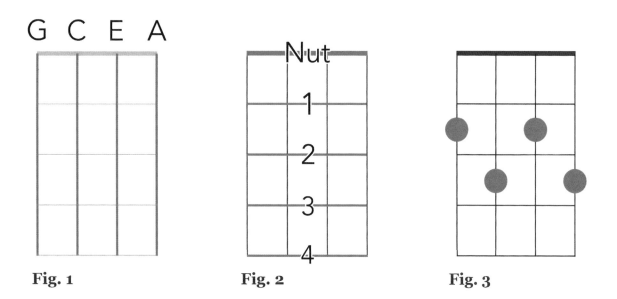

Fig. 1   Fig. 2   Fig. 3

Sometimes finger dots contain numbers. These usually show which finger to use for each note. The charts in this book don't include those hints. Use what feels comfortable; if a chord seems too hard, experiment with other fingerings. See page 11 for tips.

HOW TO READ THE CHARTS

In these chord charts, instead of showing every single chord, name, and fingering, you will find just the main foundation shapes for each chord type. They are all you need to cover the same amount of sonic ground as a traditional chord book.

Each **chord type** has its own section. You'll see notes describing its sound and usage, along with the shapes. Each shape has its own chord box as described on the previous page, but with some additional information:

- The **root** note of the chord is highlighted in red since it is the focal point of each shape (all other notes are black). If the root is a red dot, it is included as part of the fingered shape and played just like normal. Sometimes the root note *isn't* included in a chord and is shown as a red square - helpful for locating the chord, but NOT played.

- The chord's scale degrees (its **formula**) are labeled and shown below each string line in the diagram. This is useful for seeing how the notes relate to the root.

HOW TO FIND A CHORD:

1. **Pick a shape and root name.** If you want to learn how to play a G minor chord, look up a minor chord shape and remember "G" for the next step.

2. **Find the root on the fretboard.** It must be on the same string as the highlighted red root in the shape. If the note lands higher or lower on the fretboard than you need for your current application, go back to step 1 and try a different shape.

3. **Line them up.** Finger the chord shape and move it up or down the neck until the root note on the fretboard is under your finger and lined up with the root shown in the chord shape (red).

Take no notice of where the shape is within the chord box. It has nothing to do with where it should be played. The hard nut line is left out intentionally so that you can move the shape up or down easily as if on an "endless" fretboard.

Example 1:

To the right is a basic major chord shape. Perhaps you know it visually as **Bb**. Great! But forget that for now.

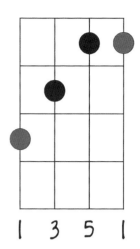

Note that the two outside dots are colored red. You will also see the *scale degrees* of each note located below the string lines. The colored dot is always the 1 - the root.

Let's say you're looking at a chart for a song that uses an F major chord, but don't want to play the simple, open shape everyone always uses. You decide on a whim that this major shape (above right) looks like it could be interesting!

The root of the chord is F, so you need to find an F note on the string where the root dot is located. In this case there are two root dots - each on an outside string: G and A. Locate the F note on each:

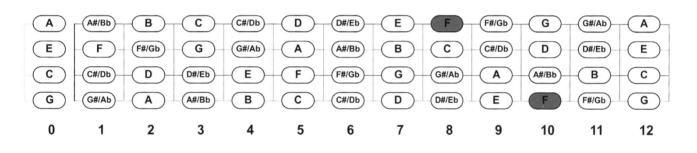

Either note works and both lead to the same result. Line the chord shape up with the F on the 8th fret and you create the chord on the right. It's an F major chord that uses the Bb shape.

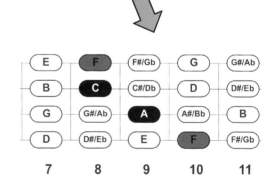

To make a C chord with this shape, just align the root dot with a C note on the proper string. There is a C on the 3rd fret of the A string. Start the shape there and it's a C.

To make a Bb, just move the shape to the 1st fret where the root lines up with a Bb note. Doesn't that look familiar?!

This works with any of the 12 notes on that string! One shape = 12 chords!

Example 2:

Here's a harder shape to work with. It's a dominant 9th. Notice the red *square*? That's the root. It's not fingered in the shape, but still vital to finding where you're at.

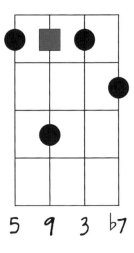

For kicks, let's pretend we're playing the jazz/swing classic, *All of Me* and want to use this shape for a couple of the chords in the song. (You know, to spice things up!) In the key of C, A9, D9, and G9 are all great **substitutions** for jazzing up the standard 7th chords with the same root.

The first step is to find the three root notes on the C string, since that's where the red square is:

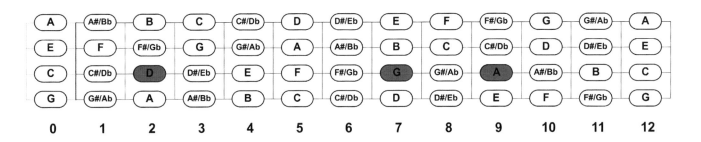

D is on the 2nd fret, G is on the 7th fret, A is on the 9th fret. Align the red root square in the shape with these notes and you end up with three hip 9th chords - D9, G9, and A9, from left to right:

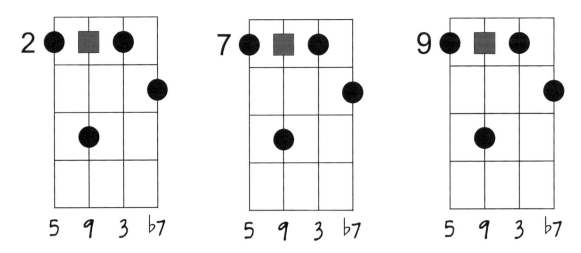

Note the fret number to the left of each chord box. It shows what fret the box should start on to create the correct sound on your 'ukulele. For example, on the left, D9, has a "2" next to it. That means to start the diagram as shown from the 2nd fret.

INVERSIONS

If one chord shape puts your fingers way up the neck and you want to stay in a lower register, try a different **inversion** – or shape. And vice versa.

The shapes in Chapter 2 are organized in order of inversion (see Chapter 3 for the juicy details). The lowest inversion of the shape is in the leftmost column. Head to the right and the shapes cycle through higher inversions. All things being equal, the shapes will climb up the fretboard as you move left to right.

Depending on the root, the shapes on either the high or low end may jump up or down an octave and fall out of line. Low to high/left to right is a good guideline for finding shapes in a range where they are most useful to you, though.

FINGERINGS

The one thing that these chord charts don't show are suggested fingerings. And it's for that exact reason: fingerings are *suggested*. They aren't law. Everyone's body is different and the physical action of holding a chord should adjust accordingly.

That said, there are generally accepted fingerings for many chords and you can, of course, finger shapes incorrectly. Usually fingering a chord the "wrong way" over-stresses your hand, arm, and shoulder (also your neck and back and... you get the idea).

Here are some tips that work in many (but not all) cases for figuring out a fingering:

- ♣ Lower numbered fingers on lower frets. Fretting fingers are numbered: index=1, middle=2, ring=3, and pinky=4.

- ♣ When you need to play the same fret on several strings, lower numbered fingers go closer to the ceiling on the higher-numbered strings (G=4, C=3, E=2, A=1).

- ♣ Two or more notes that live next to each other on the same fret might benefit from a **barre** - covering the notes with one finger. Often a barre works best on adjacent strings, but if the barre is lower than other fingers, non-adjacent strings can also work.

- ♣ If it seems contorted, it probably is - try again! There's a big difference between a difficult fingering and a hopelessly tangled one.

2

The Charts

The following charts are the heart of this book. They are organized by family: **major**, **minor**, **dominant**, **suspended**, **add**, **diminished**, and **augmented** - a rough order of usefulness and popularity (or lack thereof).

Each family has chords that can be described with the parent, umbrella name. Major 7th, major 6th, and major 7#5 chords are filed under MAJOR. Minor 6th, minor 7th, and minor major 7th are filed under MINOR. Dominant 7th, 9th, and 13th chords are filed under DOMINANT. You get the idea...

MAJOR

The following chord types all contain major intervals that provide an open, uplifting, and happy sound. I think of them as the light side of music. They are ordered from very common to "what the heck is that?!"

MAJOR
Formula: 1 3 5 • **Symbol:** [no symbol], M, maj, Δ, MA

The major chord is the most common chord in Western music. It provides much of the movement we hear in everything from pop to classical music.

There are three main *closed* major shapes (see pg. 47-48 for more on closed chords):

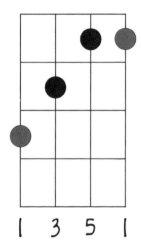 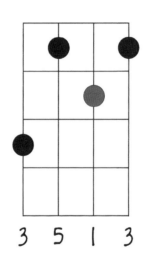 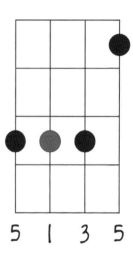

Remove a note from either side and you get two *triads* out of each (see pg. 49 for triads):

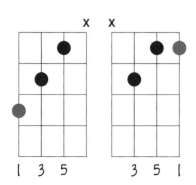 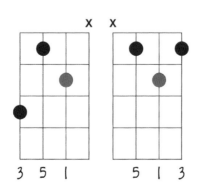 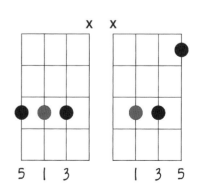

OPEN MAJOR CHORDS

There are even more variations when you create **open** major chords - chords that span more than an octave in range. In fact, the only limiting factor to how many open shapes there are is how far your fingers can stretch! Shown here are some common voicings that fit inside four frets.

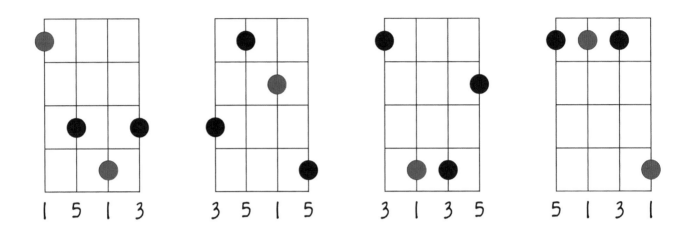

Each of the above open shapes can be reduced to a minimalistic three-string chord. Because of the absence of a doubled note, these open triads have a great, pure sound.

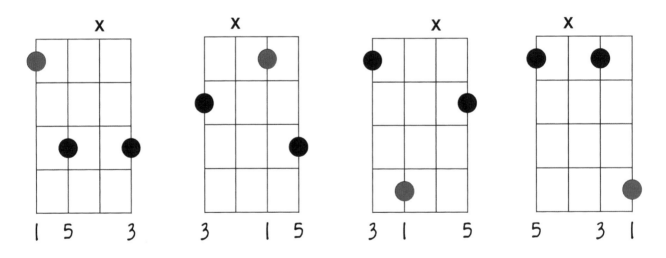

The two middle triad shapes use the same notes and sound identical, but are played differently. Each has its place in an arrangement depending on where you are going or where you are coming from. Match these with their minor counterparts for great ascending or descending chord sequences.

MAJOR 6TH
Formula: 1 3 5 6 • **Symbol:** 6, M6, Δ6, maj6, MA6

These are great substitution chords. The added tonalities, if used to substitute plain **I IV V** major chords, don't clash so you don't have to worry about notes "fitting."

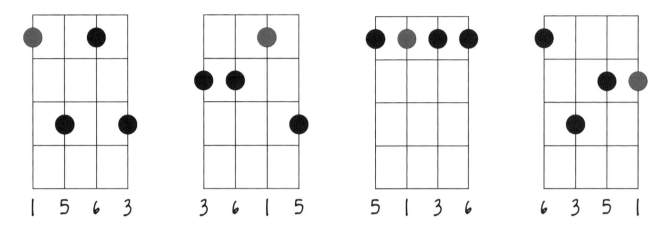

| 1 5 6 3 | 3 6 1 5 | 5 1 3 6 | 6 3 5 1 |

MAJOR 6/9
Formula: 1 3 5 6 9 • **Symbol:** 6/9, M6/9, Δ6/9, maj6/9, MA6/9

Here's one of my favorites! It spans the sonic middle ground between a jazz harmony and a wide-open suspended or add chord. Try ending a tune with one of these!

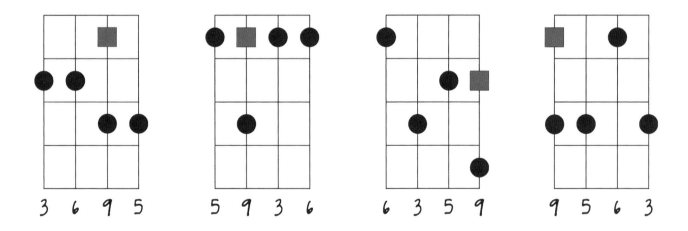

| 3 6 9 5 | 5 9 3 6 | 6 3 5 9 | 9 5 6 3 |

Bonus: Treat the "5" as if it was the root note and these 6/9 chords will function as a secondary shape that omits the 3rd instead of the root. Having different variations on formula structure can create some neat-sounding results with these extended chords.

MAJOR 7TH
Formula: 1 3 5 7 • **Symbol:** `maj7, M7, Δ7, MA7`

This chord type is heavily used in jazz, but fits anywhere you need a very mellow but complex sound. Great substitution for the **I** or **IV** chord (but NOT the **V**!).

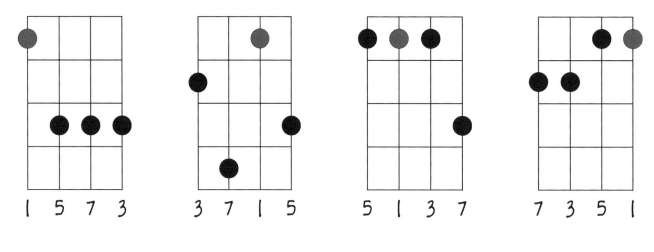

MAJOR 7 (FLAT 5TH)
Formula: 1 3 b5 7 • **Symbol:** `maj7(b5), M7(b5), Δ7b5, MA7b5`

Here's a weird one you would use when playing really far-out jazz or when looking for a gnarly passing chord in a solo arrangement.

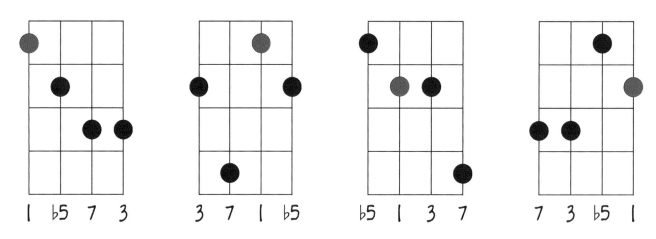

There's only one note that is different between the major 7th and major 7th (flat 5) shapes. Can you find it? Being able to visually compare chord structure like this will greatly speed up your study as you learn similar shapes.

MAJOR 7TH (SHARP 5TH)
Formula: 1 3 #5 7 • **Symbol:** `maj7(#5)`, `M7(#5)`, `MA7#5`, `Δ7#5`, `maj+7`, `Δ+7`

Another goofy one! This chord is also known as an "augmented major seventh" because of the
#5 interval. (A #5 interval is known as an augmented 5th.)

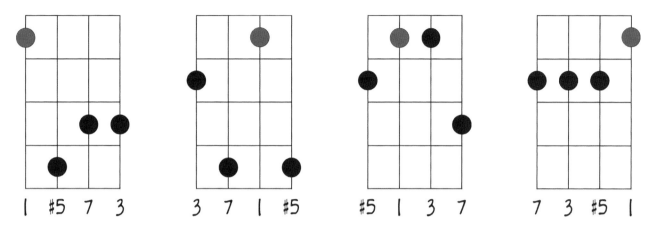

| | #5 | 7 | 3 | | 3 | 7 | | #5 | | #5 | | 3 | 7 | | 7 | 3 | #5 | |

MAJOR 9TH
Formula: 1 3 5 7 9 • **Symbol:** `maj9`, `M9`, `MA9`, `Δ9`

This one should look familiar! Its the same shape as a major 6th. However, the usage is as a
beefed-up, fancy major 7th. The red square signifies the root, but is not played.

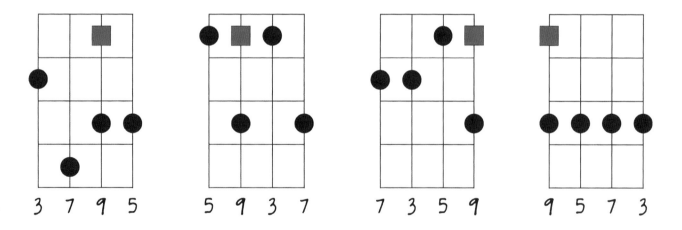

| 3 | 7 | 9 | 5 | | 5 | 9 | 3 | 7 | | 7 | 3 | 5 | 9 | | 9 | 5 | 7 | 3 |

Tip: To facilitate easier memorizing, you can think of a major 9th as a major 7th shape with
the root raised two frets. See, look! If you replace the 9th degree of the chord with the red
root square it's exactly the same shape as a major 7th.

MINOR

This section is home to chords containing a minor 3rd interval (a flat 3rd). They sound darker and more sad than chords found other places.

MINOR

Formula: 1 b3 5 • Symbol: `m, -, min`

The backdrop sound of every standoff in a Western movie, every jump scare in a horror film, and every scene in which the dog dies can usually be credited to a minor chord or two.

Same as with major chords, there are three closed minor shapes:

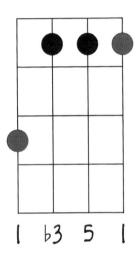

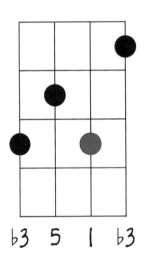

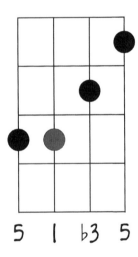

Here are the triads from each:

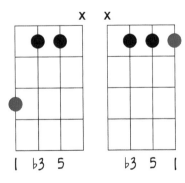

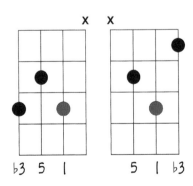

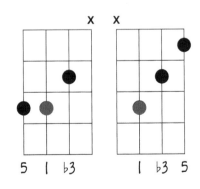

OPEN MINOR CHORDS

Open minor chords stretch a little further than their major counterparts. Here are a handful:

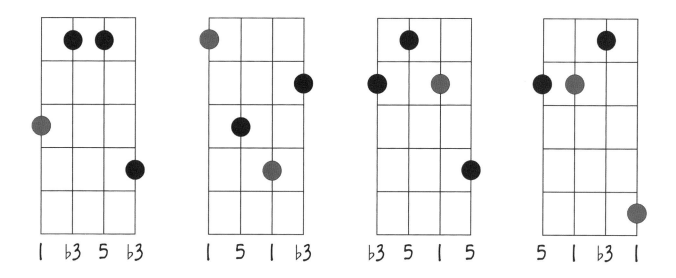

And if you strip them down to bare triads they appear to get even harder to play!

The second and third are the most useful of the open minor shapes, but it's good to have options. (The first two are the same note-wise, just different shapes.)

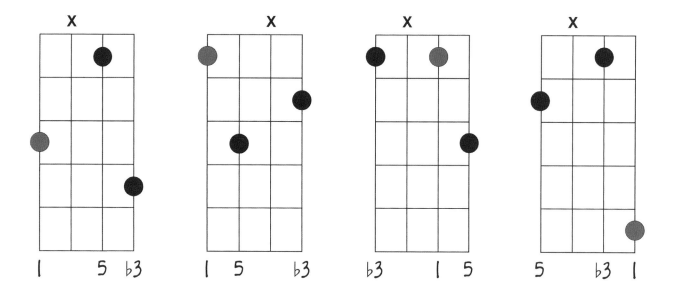

MINOR 6TH
Formula: `1 b3 5 6` • **Symbol:** `m6, -6, min6`

The first of our more interesting minor chords. These minor 6th chords are kind of odd because, while they have the **b3** that makes them minor, the **6** note is unaltered, making them sound funny in many places you'd expect a normal minor chord to go.

Try using this one as a substitute for a **ii** chord (minor 2) in a jazz progression.

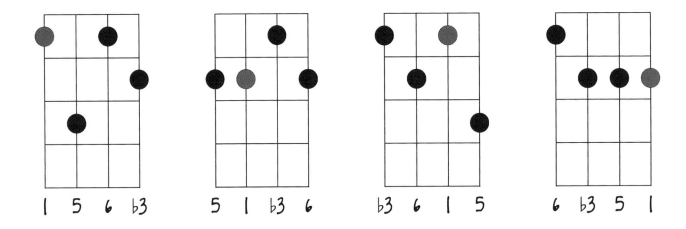

MINOR 6/9
Formula: `1 b3 5 6 9` • **Symbol:** `m6/9, -6/9, min6/9`

Here is the minor counterpart to the great-sounding major 6/9. It just adds a 9th chord tone to the minor 6th shown above. Like most chords with five or more tones, we'll leave out the root.

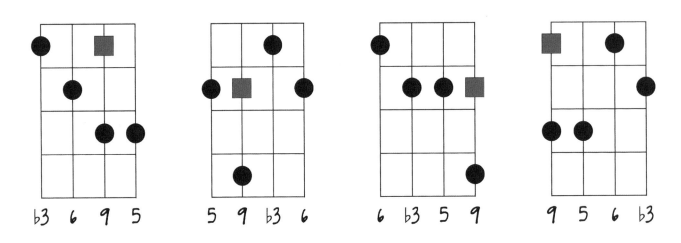

MINOR 7TH
Formula: `1 b3 5 b7` • **Symbol:** `m7, -7, min7`

Here's the common minor substitution-equivalent of a major 6th (they use the same shape!). A minor 7th works as an alternate chord for any of the minor chords in a key.

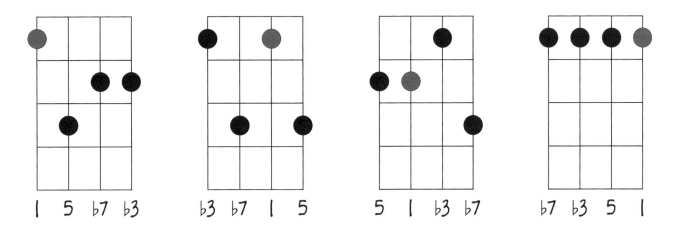

Since it uses the same shape as a major 6th, you can think of a minor 7th as a major 6th shape with the root on the 6th note. On the other hand, a major 6th is a minor 7th with the root on the b3 note.

MINOR 7TH (FLAT 5)
Formula: `1 b3 b5 b7` • **Symbol:** `m7b5, m7(b5), -7b5, min7b5, ø7`

This is a common jazz chord also known as a half-diminished seventh. It's often notated by a circle with a slash through it, like this: `Cø7` (same as `Cm7b5`). It's commonly used in place of the `ii` chord leading to a `V7b9`.

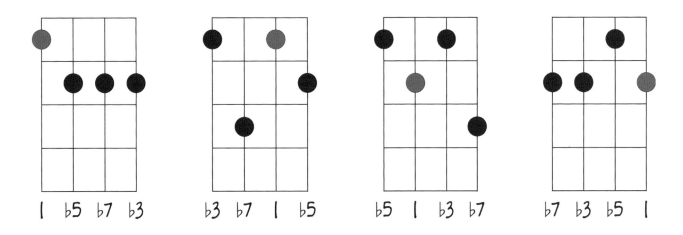

MINOR 7TH (SHARP 5TH)
Formula: `1 b3 #5 b7` • **Symbol:** `m7#5, m7(#5), -7#5, min7#5`

A pretty sounding chord by itself. Too bad its function is as a minor - weird!

It looks the same as an add9 (found later in the book).

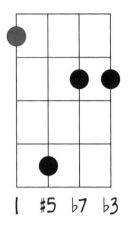
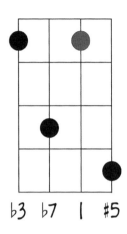
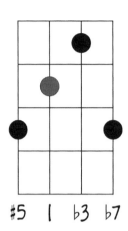
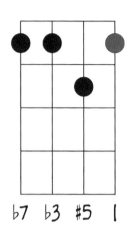

MINOR MAJOR 7TH
Formula: `1 b3 5 7` • **Symbol:** `mM7, m/M7, m(M7), min/maj7, m(maj7), -maj7`

Here's a very dissonant chord. The minor major 7th chord's signature sound comes from its major 7th interval (as opposed to the **b7** that is common in the minor family).

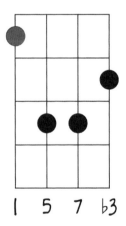
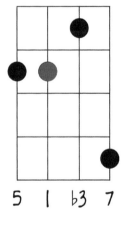
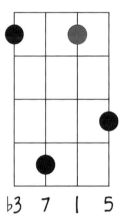
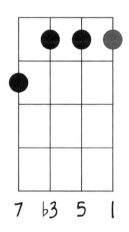

Think about this: Every chord is made up of notes - individual voices. What would happen if you played them separately through a chord progression and examined what the movement was on just the A string, just the E string, etc...?

MINOR 9TH
Formula: `1 b3 5 b7 9` • **Symbol:** `m9, -9, min9`

In this chord we've omitted the root note (shown in red for reference). It's basically a more complex-sounding minor 7th chord that takes the shape of a major 7th.

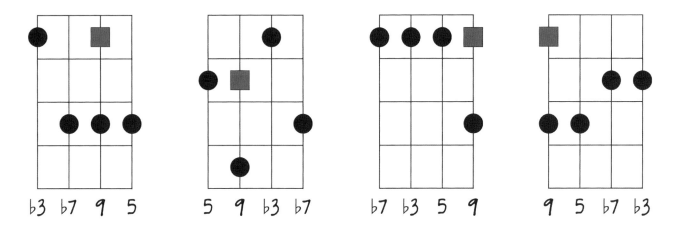

MINOR 11TH
Formula: `1 b3 5 b7 9 11` • **Symbol:** `m11, -11, min11`

This chord once again adds another sonic extension to the basic minor sound.

The minor 11 looks like a 6/9.

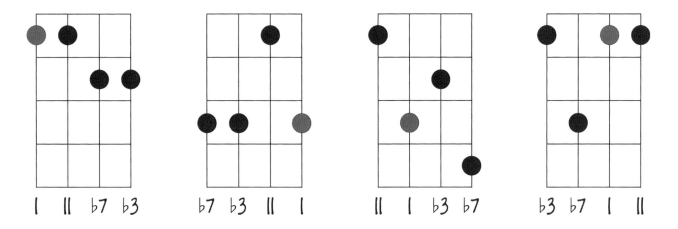

Perspective: These extra-fancy chords are great, but keep it real when assessing whether to use one or not. Many times a simpler shape will do the job better. Just because it's there doesn't mean you have to use it.

DOMINANT

Music is all about tension and release. A song that has only one chord is going to sound fairly stagnant by Western standards. That's why we use chord changes to create movement - push and pull. The kings of the sonic "pull" are the chords in the dominant family.

A characteristic of a dominant chord is the inclusion of something called the **tritone**. This tritone thing is made up of three whole steps in a row (a **#4** interval). It sounds nasty when played by itself. Try it: play F on the 1st fret, E string and B on the 2nd fret, A string at the same time. That's a tritone and it is a *sour* sound!

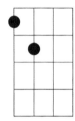 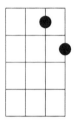

Included in a chord however, it can be quite pleasing, as you will see in this section. All of the following chord types have a built-in tritone. Just look for the signature angled interval shape on the G/C strings and the E/A strings shown above.

DOMINANT 7TH
Formula: 1 3 5 b7 • **Symbol:** 7, dom7

With a signature "bluesy" twang, dominant 7th chords are the workhorses in many places in popular music, pushing and pulling your ear to the next place.

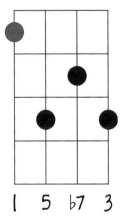 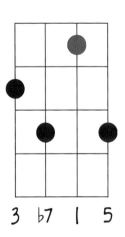 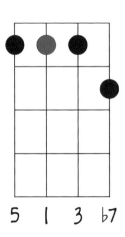 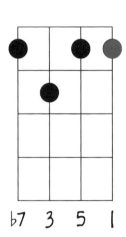

| 1 5 b7 3 | 3 b7 1 5 | 5 1 3 b7 | b7 3 5 1 |

DOMINANT 7TH (FLAT 5)
Formula: 1 3 b5 b7 • Symbol: 7b5, 7(b5)

Some way, somehow, when you flat the **5** of each dominant 7th chord shape, it creates two identical shapes. Remember where the two root locations are for each shape and you've cut your workload in half!

Also note the *double* tritones! I think this can be filed under "super gnarly, dude."

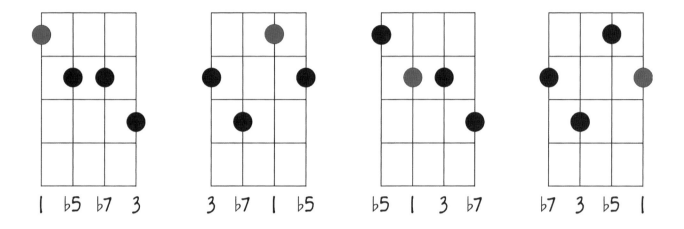

| 1 b5 b7 3 | 3 b7 1 b5 | b5 1 3 b7 | b7 3 b5 1 |

DOMINANT 7TH (SHARP 5)
Formula: 1 3 #5 b7 • Symbol: 7#5, 7(#5), aug7, +7

The **5** in the 7#5 chord moves in the opposite direction of the previous chord type. It is fairly common in jazz tunes. While it sounds and looks difficult, it's really pretty easy to figure out on the fly - just move the 5th of a dominant 7th up one fret!

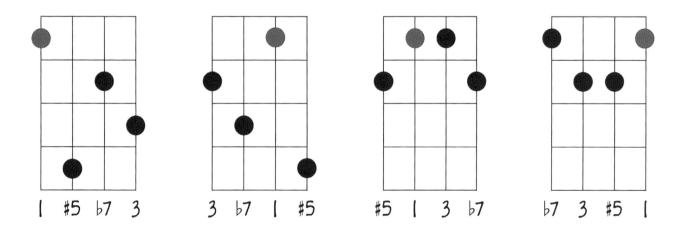

| 1 #5 b7 3 | 3 b7 1 #5 | #5 1 3 b7 | b7 3 #5 1 |

DOMINANT 7TH (FLAT 9)
Formula: 1 3 5 b7 b9 • **Symbol:** 7b9, 7(b9)

Making four diagrams for this repeating shape is pretty redundant, but maybe somebody somewhere really wants to know where the **3** is in each iteration of a 7b9 chord. For those less ambitious, just know that a 7b9 is a diminished 7th shape, but the root is located one fret down from what is actually played.

Or you could think of it like a 7th chord with the root moved up one fret.

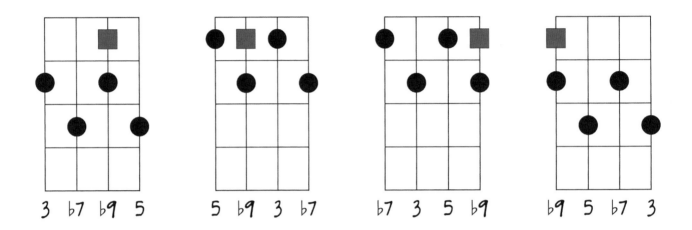

3 b7 b9 5   5 b9 3 b7   b7 3 5 b9   b9 5 b7 3

DOMINANT 7TH (SHARP 9)
Formula: 1 3 5 b7 #9 • **Symbol:** 7#9, 7(#9)

AKA "The Hendrix Chord." This sweet and sour chord was popularized by its use in Jimi's *Purple Haze* and *Foxy Lady*. The 7#9 contains both the major 3rd and the minor 3rd (the **#9** is the same as a minor 3rd) which gives it a nasty sound.

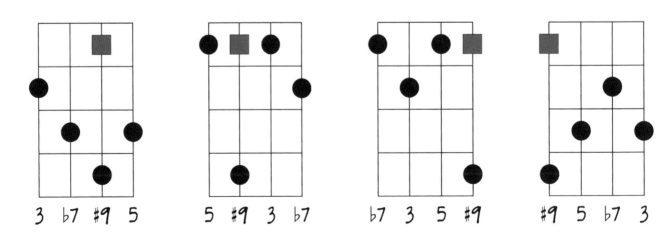

3 b7 #9 5   5 #9 3 b7   b7 3 5 #9   #9 5 b7 3

DOMINANT 9TH
Formula: 1 3 5 b7 9 • Symbol: 9

When you need a sharp-dressed 7th chord, reach for a 9th. It's a staple of jazz standards and targets key juicy tones on the 'ukulele without sitting too far out in left field like some other extended chords.

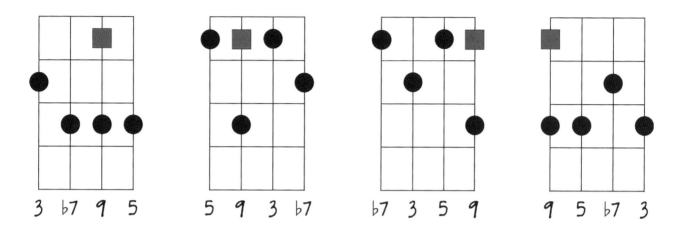

DOMINANT 11TH
Formula: 1 3 5 b7 9 11 • Symbol: 11

Add a tone to the 9th chord and you get an 11th. More sonic juiciness.

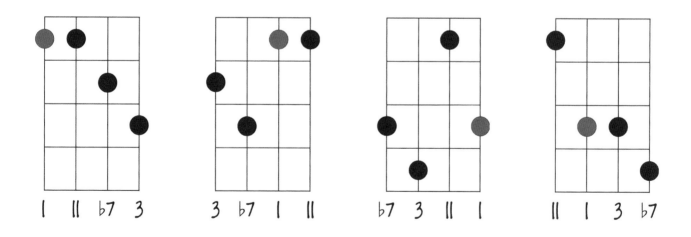

Moving voices: When switching chords it can be helpful to imagine each string as a voice in a choir. How many voices move in the chord change? Sometimes you want them all to move. Sometimes you want as few as possible to move. Case in point: *One Note Samba* - a great example of effective "minimalist" chord movements.

DOMINANT 13TH
Formula: 1 3 5 b7 9 11 13 • **Symbol:** 13

Now *this* chord is abstract. The 13th is the largest chord in this book as far as note-count goes. Because of that it has more omissions. No matter how weird it sounds, you will still find it on jazz charts and that's why it's here. Otherwise, you've got to be looking for trouble to reach for one of these!

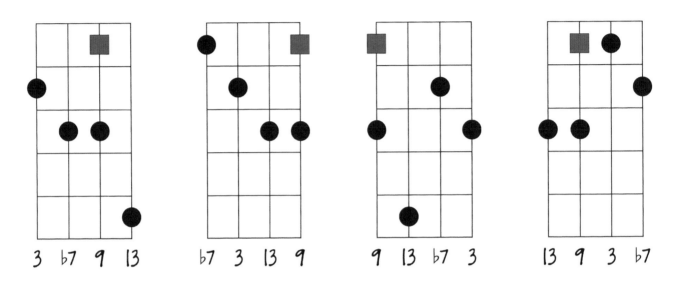

3 b7 9 13   b7 3 13 9   9 13 b7 3   13 9 3 b7

DOMINANT 13TH (FLAT 9)
Formula: 1 3 5 b7 b9 11 13 • **Symbol:** 13b9

By moving the 9th tone of a dominant 13 chord down one fret, you end up with a pretty funky shape. Pairing the **b7** and **13** tones makes for a really dissonant sound.

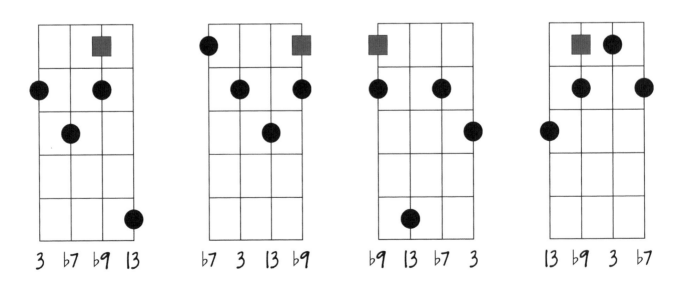

3 b7 b9 13   b7 3 13 b9   b9 13 b7 3   13 b9 3 b7

ALTERED
Formula: 1 3 b5-*or*-#5 b7 b9-*or*-#9 • **Symbol:** `Alt, b5/#5 b9/#9`

No charts here, just a description of a funny, variable chord type. An altered chord is pretty much a 9th chord, but one that is expanded by mandatory changes to key chord tones. Both the **5** *and* the **9** tones **must** be either flat or sharp in an altered chord - neither can be natural. For example, G7#5b9, A7b5b9, or C#7b5#9 are all altered chords, even though their chord suffix doesn't match.

Many times altered chords are notated as "G7alt" in lead sheets.

My favorite thing about altered chords is that you have choices when selecting which one you play. It's like the musician's union of chords! (Well, maybe not...) But still, feel like sharpening the **5** and flattening the **9**? Great! Feel like sharpening both? Great! Feel like flattening the **5** and sharpening the **9**? Great! All will work in harmony to some degree or another and you get to choose which variation to play.

On the 'ukulele, some transformations happen when you make certain alterations:

- Flattening both the **5** and **9** creates a dominant 7th chord shape (not of the same root, unfortunately).

- Sharpening the **5** and flattening the **9** creates a dominant 9th shape (also not related).

Make sure you've got a strong grasp on your 9th chords and then start playing around with changing both the **5** and **9** tones to create altered variations.

SUSPENDED

A suspended chord happens when you shift the third tone of a chord up or down to a **2** or **4**. It has a big, lush, and open sound (think: The Police) because it's neither major or minor (which the absent third delineates). You can make pretty much any chord suspended by moving the third, but here are some of the most common types.

SUSPENDED 2

Formula: 1 2 5 • **Symbol:** sus2, 2

Suspended 2 and suspended 4 chords are interesting because they each use the same shapes - the same *seven* shapes, I might add - but with different roots. This gives you plenty of options for playing these great-sounding grips!

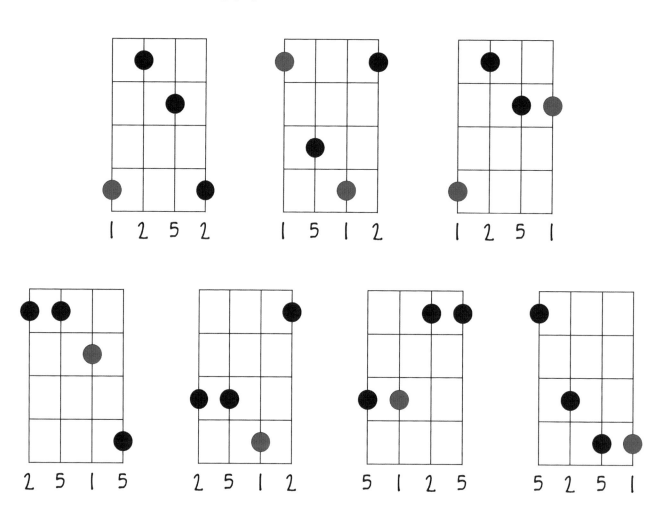

SUSPENDED 4

Formula: 1 4 5 • **Symbol:** sus4, 4

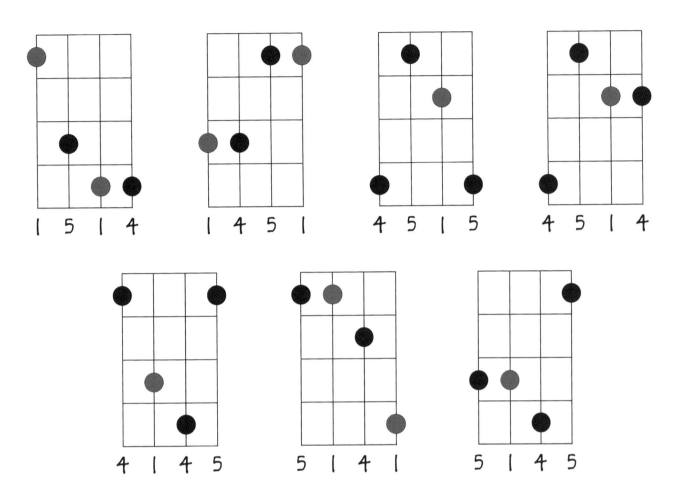

1 5 1 4   1 4 5 1   4 5 1 5   4 5 1 4

4 1 4 5   5 1 4 1   5 1 4 5

SUSPENDED 7th

Formula: 1 4 5 ♭7 • **Symbol:** 7sus, 7sus4, sus7

Just a 7th chord with the third pushed up to a fourth. Looks like a major 6/9.

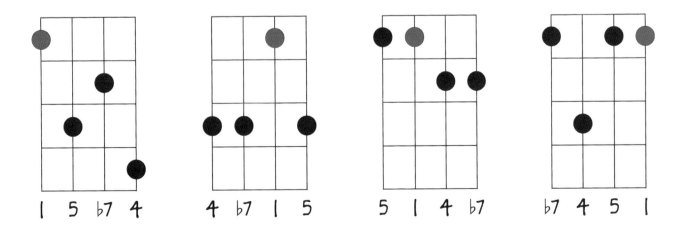

1 5 ♭7 4   4 ♭7 1 5   5 1 4 ♭7   ♭7 4 5 1

ADD

Add chords are related to suspended chords, but retain the major 3rd tonality for a major feel. A sweet, non-committal sound that can skew the current chord in an unexpected direction, usually without any collateral damage.

Just like it sounds, either a **9** or **11** tone is added to a major chord. But because the **9** is really the **2** and the **11** is really the **4**, the names are often interchangable.

ADD9/ADD2
Formula: 1 3 5 9 • **Symbol:** add9, add2

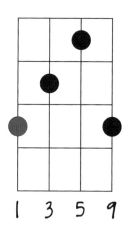

1 3 5 9

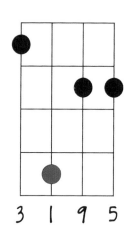

3 1 9 5

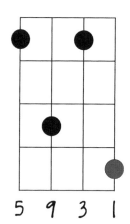

5 9 3 1

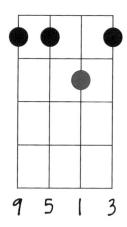

9 5 1 3

ADD11/ADD4
Formula: 1 3 5 11 • **Symbol:** add11, add4

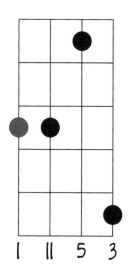

1 11 5 3

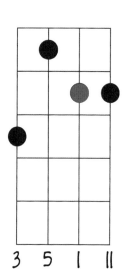

3 5 1 11

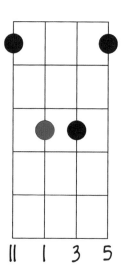

11 1 3 5

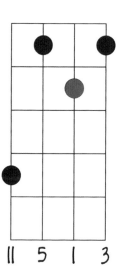

11 5 1 3

DIMINISHED

The diminished family is small - only two chord types - and has an odd sound and even odder fingerings. Widely used as transition chords, you won't find many songs that use the diminished sound as a foundation tonality.

DIMINISHED

Formula: 1 b3 b5 • **Symbol:** dim, °

The plain, run-of-the-mill diminished triad is a minor chord with a **b5**. It creates a bluesy sort of sound and if you look closely, you might recognize some tritonian fragments in the shapes that resemble 7th chords.

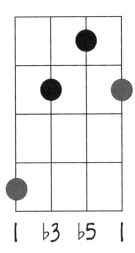

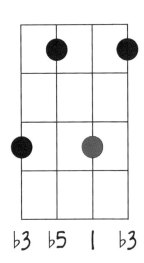

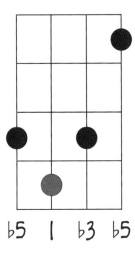

You can break them into triads like this:

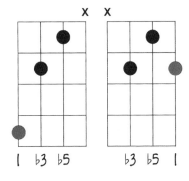

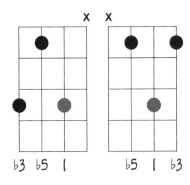

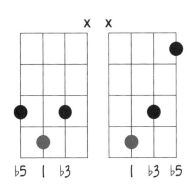

OPEN DIMINISHED CHORDS

There are two obvious open diminished triad shapes. Others are a stretch - and really, when are you going to use them?

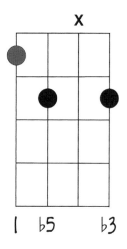

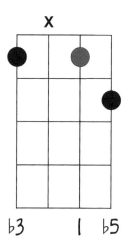

DIMINISHED 7TH
Formula: `1 b3 b5 bb7` • **Symbol:** `Dim7, °7`

Of the two diminished shapes, I find the diminished 7th most practical because it's easier to remember and sounds just as good, if not better, in every situation I've ever needed a diminished chord.

All you've got to remember is that every note contained in this shape can be the root name.

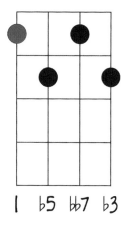

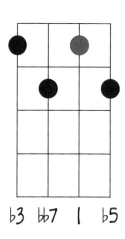

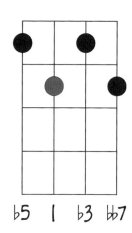

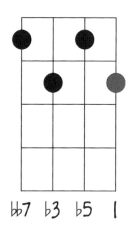

AUGMENTED

This page is near the end of the chapter for a very good reason: augmented chords are a rare breed! They sound really weird and therefore are hard to use. Not too many people are brave enough to disturb their listeners with an augmented chord! That said, it's one of the four main triads so deserves its place.

AUGMENTED
Formula: 1 3 #5 • Symbol: aug, +

The cookie crumbles in a symmetrical way when you play an augmented chord on the 'ukulele. Because of that, every note in each shape is a root. The chord repeats every time you move up four frets (not counting where you start).

CLOSED:

OPEN:

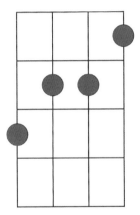

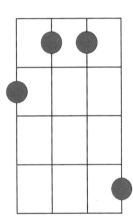

TRIADS:

OPEN TRIADS:

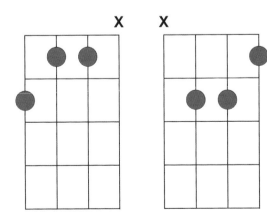

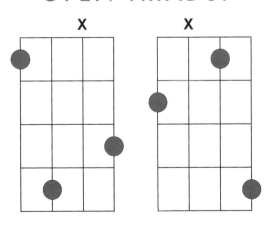

SLASH CHORDS

Keyboard players have it easy. They can morph a basic chord into something that sounds complex by adding a different bass note. Play an A minor with your right hand, plop a D in with your left, and bam! With very little extra effort you end up with a D9 of sorts. This shortcut chord/bass note relation is called a ***slash chord***.

While they are easy to use on keyboard, slash chords are a huge pain in the neck on 'ukulele. If you see one, run the other way! You can tell when you've met the enemy by the slash down the middle of a chord and a note, like this: C/B, Gm/A, etc... On the left is the foundation chord. It's very often a simple triad. To the right of the slash is the bass note.

> When you are saying it aloud, a slash chord is vocalized: *"[chord] over [note]"* or *"[chord] with a [note] in the bass."*

The bass note in a slash chord is lower in pitch than the rest of the chord. Period. That's the reason a slash chord functions as it does. Move that bass tone above another note and it completely changes the chord. Sometimes this is used to highlight certain voicings of a simple chord. You see slash chords like G/B a lot. It's just a 1st inversion G major with a B in the bass that the composer wants to highlight.

There are two approaches to playing slash chords on the 'ukulele:

1. Playing them correctly with the bass as the lowest note.

2. Playing them incorrectly with the bass somewhere other than the bottom.

Because it's more simple, I'll give a brief overview of the "wrong way" first. This is easiest and most straightforward when the foundation chord is a triad. When this is the case, find the bare triad on three of the strings and look for the "bass" note on the leftover string. Shuffle your way through triad shapes until you find one that has the bass note as a playable and convenient neighbor.

To "cheat" a more complex slash chord with four notes, you can use any string for the "bass" note - just slap it in there! The sound will change depending on what note you replace, so if it doesn't work at first, try a different option.

Keeping the bass as the lowest note and doing things the "right" way is easiest on a low-G strung 'ukulele. The bass note will always be on the lowest string. On a high-G uke, the bass note lands on the C string, which makes the shapes much more awkward.

Here are some examples for the purists who want to play slash chords the right way:

C/B

C major with a B in the Bass. Put B on the G string, 4th fret – there is your bass note. The trick is now to find a C major triad on the three highest strings while staying within fretting distance of the B. Refer to the major triad shapes to see some options. I'd probably use: **4433**, a 3rd inversion C major 7th chord.

Em/C

Because there are already two G notes in an open Em chord (**0432**), the open G string can be used for the bass note very easily. Add the C note on the 5th fret of the top string. Guess what?! It's C major 7th again, albeit one that uses a different shape – **5432**.

G7/A

This one is harder because a four-note 7th chord already uses up all of the 'ukulele's strings. To add a fifth note to mix we would need five strings! That means to fit the A in there, one note from the **G7** needs to go. You can usually get away with removing the root from a big chord, so I would take away the open G and replace it with the A bass note. This is a G9 chord without a root - **2212**.

<u>Other options for handling slash chords:</u>

1. Don't worry about it! Play the chord shown to the left of the slash and call it a day. It will be close enough.

2. Hire a bass player.

3. Buy your keyboardist friend a six-pack of beer and ask him or her to re-write the chart in plain English.

3

How Chords Work

If the shapes in the last chapter left you curious about chord theory, keep reading. What follows is an explanation of how chords work.

It is not necessary to understand what makes a chord tick and if the idea really bores you, feel free to skip over this chapter. However, understanding chords will inform your musical outlook in the long run. I'll even go as far as to say that I would be surprised if some major lightbulbs don't flash on for you in the next few pages if this is your first look into the subject.

BUILDING A CHORD

A chord is built using two pieces of information: a **scale** and a *formula*. The scale tells you the family of notes you are working with and the formula tells you which family members to select.

STEP 1: FIND THE ROOT SCALE

Chords are always built with a **major** scale. *Which* major scale is determined by the root name of the chord you wish to create. For example:

- Cm is built from a C major scale
- A is built from an A major scale
- Ebm7#5 is built from an Eb scale

Always use a major scale, no matter what crazy name the chord might have.

For reference, here are all 12 major scales. You will notice that some use sharps and some use flats. For scales that have a natural root (without a # or b), this is fixed. For those that don't (Bb, C#, Eb, F#, Ab), you can theoretically use enharmonic equivalents to change flats to sharps and vice-versa. An enharmonic equivalent is the same note, called two different things (Bb is the same as A#). The most common version of each key is shown here.

A	B	C#	D	E	F#	G#	A
Bb	C	D	Eb	F	G	A	Bb
B	C#	D#	E	F#	G#	A#	B
C	D	E	F	G	A	B	C
C#	D#	E#	F#	G#	A#	B#	C#
D	E	F#	G	A	B	C#	D
Eb	F	G	Ab	Bb	C	D	Eb
E	F#	G#	A	B	C#	D#	E
F	G	A	Bb	C	D	E	F
F#	G#	A#	B	C#	D#	E#	F#
G	A	B	C	D	E	F#	G
Ab	Bb	C	Db	Eb	F	G	Ab

STEP 2: NUMBER THE SCALE

When you find the correct major scale for the chord you wish to build, write it out. If you were using a C scale it would look like this:

C D E F G A B C

Give each note an ascending number:

1 2 3 4 5 6 7 8
C D E F G A B C

The last note can be called **8** *or* **1**. Since both are the root, the **8** *is* the **1**. After that it just goes around again. For examples here I'll use "**8**."

With these numbers in place on paper or in your mind, it becomes much easier to communicate about scales without being restricted by the note names of one key. That's why they are used in making chords. A sequence of numbers can be applied to *any* scale.

Sometimes when finding the notes in a fancy jazz chord you will count past the top end of the octave (the "**8**" on the right end of the number line). This results in additional scale degrees like **9**, **11**, and **13**. It looks difficult, but it's just an extra step.

Because of the ordering of chord notes, some of these "repeat" scale tones are never used. **10**, **12**, and **14** are the same as **3**, **5**, and **7** - already used in an extended chord. So when working past the first octave you'll only ever use **9**, **11**, and **13** - the equivalent of the **2**, **4**, and **6** scale tones.

STEP 3: KNOW THE FORMULA

Each different type of chord is made up of a combination of notes. These unique note combinations are what give each chord type its signature sound. Chord "recipes" can be represented by a number formula. This formula tells you which notes from a scale you use to make a chord. (More formulas later.)

Let's start with the formula for a major chord: **1   3   5**. That means you take the first note, 3rd note, and 5th note from a numbered scale like the one above.

STEP 4: FIND THE NOTES

Let's try taking the formula from the last step and finding its notes in a scale. Use the numbered scale degrees shown in step two and cherry-pick the notes to fit the formula.

For simplicity, let's start with a C major chord and highlight the formula (**1 3 5**):

1 2 **3** 4 **5** 6 7 8
C D **E** F **G** A B C

You end up with **C**, **E**, and **G**. Those are the notes of a C major chord!

More complicated formulas use **b** and **#** signs to alter a note. The **b** means to flat the note - or lower - the pitch by a half step (one fret). The **#** means to sharp the note - or raise - the pitch by a half step (one fret). Apply them to the scale degree where they occur. For instance, the formula for a minor chord is: **1 b3 5**. The **b3** tells you to move the third scale degree down a half step from where it would be originally - from **E** to **Eb**.

Some examples with different chord types and formulas are included below. Notice how the **b** and **#** signs change the resulting notes from the major scale.

Minor (1 b3 5)

1 2 **b3** 4 **5** 6 7 8

C D **Eb** F G A B C

Diminished (1 b3 b5)

1 2 **b3** 4 **b5** 6 7 8

C D **Eb** F **Gb** A B C

Augmented (1 3 #5)

1 2 **3** 4 **#5** 6 7 8

C D **E** F **G#** A B C

STEP 5: CREATE A SHAPE

In the previous step we came up with some formula notes for a C major chord - C, E, and G. Let's take a look at the process of putting them on the 'ukulele.

As long as you fit in all of the notes, they can appear *anywhere* on the fretboard. It's up to the musician to decide which ones to use and where. No pressure or anything - there are only about a million options!

To make the process a little less intimidating, let's first look at a familiar shape: good 'ol open C (right). Let's explore what makes it tick (notes shown below each string in the diagram):

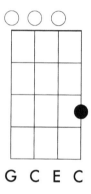

G C E C

If you look to familiar shapes for guidance in future chord-maneuvering endeavors, you will start to notice some similarities. The main similarity is that a shape has to be user-friendly. Rarely will it span more than four frets. Further than that and playability really starts to depend on the situation and player.

With "zone" thinking in mind, let's follow the breadcrumbs and see if we could find a second, higher shape for C using the same notes. Just look for the next place a C, E, or G occurs on each string.

The chord I come up with is: **5437**.

That might be great for people with stretchy fingers, but I'd rather not work that hard. Keeping the 3rd fret, A string in the same place allows for a more compact shape: **5433**.

As long as all the notes are there, the sky is the limit!

FORMULA REFERENCE CHART

So far we've only looked at the formulas for four main chords. Shown here are all the formulas for shapes included in this book - shapes that will carry you through 99.9% of musical situations. The formula for each is also included with the shapes in Chapter 2.

Major:	1 3 5
Major 6th:	1 3 5 6
Major 6/9:	1 3 5 6 9
Major 7th:	1 3 5 7
Major 7(b5):	1 3 b5 7
Major 7(#5):	1 3 #5 7
Major 9th:	1 3 5 7 9
Minor:	1 b3 5
Minor 6th:	1 b3 5 6
Minor 6/9:	1 b3 5 6 9
Minor 7th:	1 b3 5 b7
Minor 7(b5):	1 b3 b5 b7
Minor 7(#5):	1 b3 #5 b7
Minor Major 7:	1 b3 5 7
Minor 9th:	1 b3 5 b7 9
Minor 11th:	1 b3 5 b7 9 11
Dominant 7th:	1 3 5 b7
Dominant 7(b5):	1 3 b5 b7
Dominant 7(#5):	1 3 #5 b7
Dominant 7(b9)	1 3 5 b7 b9
Dominant 7(#9)	1 3 5 b7 #9
Dominant 9th:	1 3 5 b7 9
Dominant 11th:	1 3 5 b7 9 11
Dominant 13th:	1 3 5 b7 9 11 13
Dominant 13(b9):	1 3 5 b7 b9 11 13
Suspended 2:	1 2 5
Suspended 4:	1 4 5
Suspended 7th:	1 4 5 b7
Add 9:	1 3 5 9
Add 11:	1 3 5 11
Diminished:	1 b3 b5
Diminished 7th:	1 b3 b5 bb7
Augmented:	1 3 #5

PRACTICE/EXAMPLES

The name of the game here is repetition. The more chords you build, the faster and better you get at putting the pieces together. Just like anything.

To make sure you've got it, here are some additional visual examples showing how to build different chords, step-by-step. I recommend trying them by yourself first and then double-checking the examples to make sure you've arrived at the correct answer.

E7

Write out the E major scale and corresponding number line.

1	2	3	4	5	6	7	8
E	F#	G#	A	B	C#	D#	E

The formula for a dominant 7th chord is: **1 3 5 b7**. Pick those notes out of the scale and change them as needed (flat the 7):

1	2	**3**	4	**5**	6	**b7**	8
E	F#	**G#**	A	**B**	C#	**D**	E

The notes in E7 are: **E**, **G#**, **B**, and **D**. On the fretboard they show up like this:

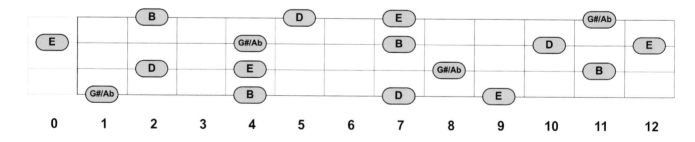

You should be able to see some obvious zones that contain all four notes. Write them out, play them, and find as many combinations as you can.

If you need to double check, look back to the charts for dominant 7th shapes in Chapter 2 and line them up with an E root.

F6/9

Write out the F major scale and the corresponding numbers.

1	2	3	4	5	6	7	8
F	G	A	Bb	C	D	E	F

Notice how the 9th extends past the "end" of the scale. You can add on extended scale tones like **9**, **11**, and **13** to get more complex harmonies.

Find the notes of the formula in the scale: **1 3 5 6 9**.

1	2	3	4	5	6	7	8	9
F	G	A	Bb	C	D	E	F	G

In this case, the **9** is really just the **2** going around again.

Find the formula notes on the fretboard:

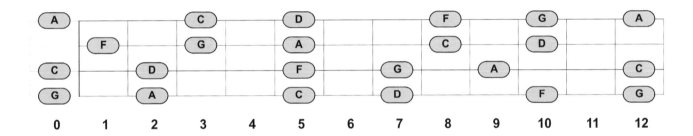

Do you see a problem? Five notes, four strings. Uh oh. Here's our first instance of **selective omitting**. Selective omitting is what I call the dropping of one or more or the notes of a chord to fit it on the 'ukulele. (This is explored in depth later.)

In this case we'll drop the root (**F**) since it is of the least importance to the sound of the chord. Now we are down to: **G, A, C,** and **D**.

Finding the shapes through the static is a bit harder for this example so I'll give you some help. Try it yourself first, then take a peek (one is missing - find it!):

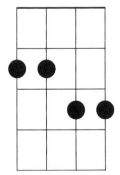
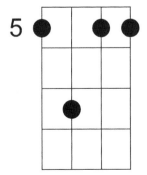
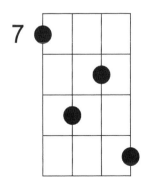

C#9(#5)

Write out the C# major scale and the corresponding numbers.

1	2	3	4	5	6	7	8
C#	D#	E#	F#	G#	A#	B#	C#

For this chord we'll use the formula for a 9th chord: **1 3 5 b7 9**. The parenthesis in the chord name are additional directions to be applied along with the main formula and notes.

To break it down, let's find the plain 9th chord notes first:

1	2	3	4	5	6	b7	8	9
C#	D#	E#	F#	G#	A#	B	C#	D#

Now use the directions in the parenthesis and sharp the **5**. **G#** goes up to **A**:

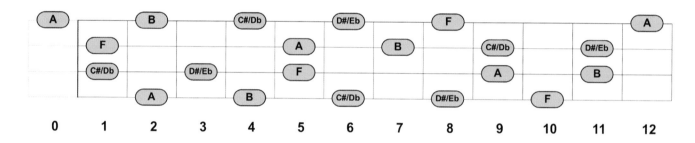

Again, there are too many notes to fit on the 'ukulele so we've got to drop one. Take out the root and we are down to **E#, A, Bb,** and **D#**. Find some playable shapes! Look at the 9(#5) shapes chart in Chapter 2 for the answers.

Notice the **E#** and **B#** in the above C# scale. They shouldn't exist, right? Wrong. In "official music" you are not supposed to write out a scale with the same letter name working for two notes (**F** and **F#**, **B** and **Bb**, etc...). For this reason the **E** becomes an **E#** due to an **F#** already in use. Same for the **B#**.

If I was the conductor type I might even call the **#5 A** note a **Gx** (double sharp) since there is already an **A#**, but that is overkill for this book. Absolute note names are much more practical, but in case you were curious, there you go. This explains why you see **E#** in the formula and **F** on the fretboard - even my scale generator doesn't want to go there!

INVERSIONS

You can think of the notes in a chord as playing cards. If you shuffle the "deck," you rearrange the notes into different chord shapes - also called *voicings* or *inversions*.

The most basic version of a chord is called the *root inversion*. This is when the root is the lowest note in the chord and the other chord tones are stacked above it in order, lowest to highest. So in a C major chord (as shown below in the leftmost note stack), you'll have **1**, **3**, **5** in order.

To create subsequent inversions, move the lowest note in the previous inversion up one octave so that it becomes the highest note in the chord stack. This exposes the **3** on the bottom and creates the *1st inversion* (second to the left).

Again, to create the next inversion, move the lowest note up an octave to the highest place. Because the **5** tone is at the bottom, this is called the *2nd inversion* (second from the right).

Move the **5** up an octave to become the highest note and you return to where you started - the root inversion, just one octave higher.

If there are more notes in the chord than the three in this example, continue raising the lowest note by an octave until you return to where you started. For example, a 9th chord has five notes so it would gain an additional two inversions - a 3rd inversion and a 4th inversion. The only difference is that with some larger chords, shifting the lowest note up an octave might not necessarily put it at the top of the stack. Instead you might shuffle the note to the middle.

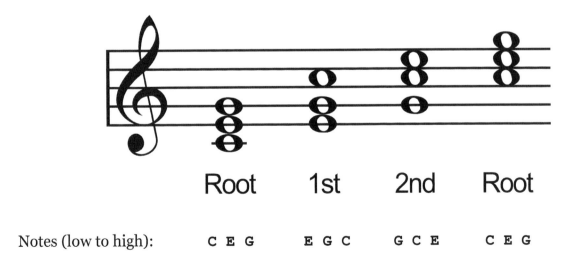

	Root	1st	2nd	Root
Notes (low to high):	C E G	E G C	G C E	C E G

47

OPEN INVERSIONS

The inversions on the previous page are all **closed**. That means that the notes in the chord fit within the range of one octave. *Keep your hands and feet inside the vehicle at all times!* The notes in an **open** chord voicing span an octave or more.

Any time you play a chord that has notes beyond a single octave it is considered "open." But since that's a little vague, let's dial it in so we have a step-by-step process for creating open voicings.

On the previous page we moved the **lowest** note of a basic triad up one octave to make subsequent closed inversions. To create open inversions out of these triads you displace the **middle** note by one octave.

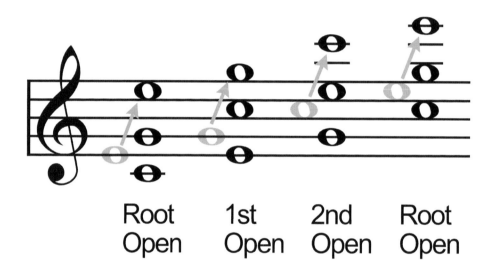

Root	1st	2nd	Root
Open	Open	Open	Open

If you examine the notes above you get:

	Root			1st			2nd			Root		
Closed:	C (E) G			E (G) C			G (C) E			C (E) G		
Open:	C	G	E	E	C	G	G	E	C	C	G	E

You can also move the middle note down an octave for several variations:

	Root			1st			2nd			Root		
Closed:	C (E) G			E (G) C			G (C) E			C (E) G		
Open:	E	C	G	G	E	C	C	G	E	E	C	G

THE "GRIP" METHOD

This book is all about chord diagrams. But it's not always possible to add a diagram box to a word document or forum post. Enter the "grip" shortcut.

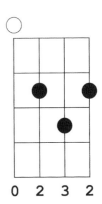

Using this method, chords are written out with four numbers in a row, like this: **0232**. Each number represents a fret on a string. Zeros are open strings. The G string is represented by the left-most number and the A string by the right. (C and E are in their respective places between.)

0232 is: open G; 2nd fret, C; 3rd fret, E; 2nd fret, A. It's a G major chord.

0 2 3 2

TRIADS AND FULL CHORDS

A chord that has only three notes in its formula is called a ***triad***. Major, minor, augmented, diminished, suspended 4, and suspended 2 chords are all triads.

Perhaps you've noticed that 'ukulele players strum all four strings *all the time*. That means when playing triad chords, there is an extra note coming from somewhere. This extra note is a doubled chord tone.

Look at an open F chord, for example: **2010**. The two outside strings are both sounding an A note - it's doubled. Same for an open D chord: **2220**.

I like to think of these triads with doubled notes as "full" versions of the chord.

This is great for filling out the sound and not having to avoid one string all the time, but you aren't playing a true triad.

Sometimes a plain triad is the best chord for the job. They have a simple, pure sound that can be very useful. Styles like funk or reggae rely heavily on bare triads so it's good to know how to play them.

There are diagrams for three string triads in Chapter 2. Study these so you know where to find the triad itself.

SELECTIVE OMITTING

A chord that uses five or more notes will not fit on the 'ukulele. It just can't be played; there are not enough strings to make all the notes sound at once! To fit some of the fancier chords on an 'ukulele we have to bring the total note count down to four.

We've already seen in the "Practice" section how the root is the most common note to omit. Even though it is the foundation note, the root is the least important to the human ear. Without it, our brain can fill in the blank.

The **5** is also a good choice for the cull for similar reasons.

CHANGING OMISSIONS

With all of that said, if you change which note you leave out, the chord will sound different. I've used commonly-accepted standard 'ukulele formulas for the chord shapes in this book, but rotate the omitted note(s) and you will create some cool new voicings.

For example, back in the last chapter, 9th chords were shown as: **3 5 b7 9**. But you could change the altered formula to something like: **1 3 b7 9** or **1 5 b7 9**. Doing this might make the chord less robust in places, but might reward you with some nice sounds that you wouldn't otherwise find.

You can also get some neat voicings by taking a chord with four or more notes and omitting all but three of them. Then you can double one scale degree as if it were a full triad.

For example, I've tried this with minor 7th shapes and ended up with chords like:

- **5213** - Dm7(no 5) with a **1 b3 b7** formula – the **b7** is doubled
- **3541** - Bbm7(no 3) with a **1 5 b7** formula – the **1** is doubled

Perhaps they aren't practical, but some of the shapes sound really sweet and could have a use somewhere. The sky is the limit!

Wrapping Up

*"The beautiful thing about learning is nobody
can take it away from you."*

~ B.B. King

You're almost to the end! Before the final pages I want to say a couple more things.

First of all, thank you for buying this book! I hope it was an informative, enjoyable read and a valuable resource for learning new chords.

If you have any questions at all, shoot me an email at `liveukulele@gmail.com`.

My website, `liveukulele.com`, is constantly being updated with free content, including lessons, song sheets, interviews, and much more. I'd love to see you there!

The next few pages include fretboard charts, a recommended reading list, a glossary, and a bit about me.

Catch you on the inter-webs or at a show!

Aloha,

Brad Bordessa

Standard: G C E A

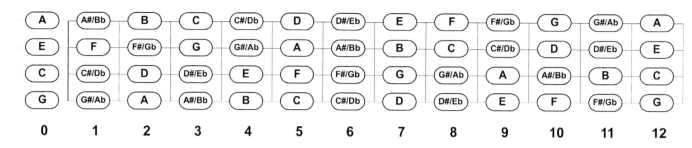

Baritone: D G B E

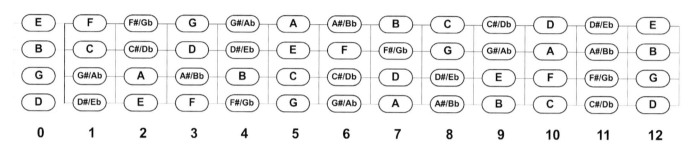

English: A D F# B

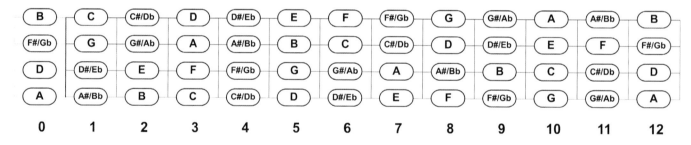

Tenor: F Bb D G

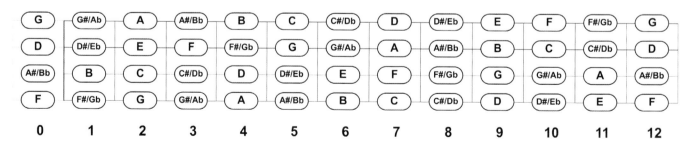

For big, giant .png versions of these charts, go to: liveukulele.com/fretboard-charts/.

RECOMMENDED RESOURCES

Here are some great resources I've fallen in love with over the years. None of them are 'ukulele-specific, but approached with an open mind, they will teach you much.

The Chord Factory

By Jon Damien

A super in-depth look at constructing chords and a step-by-step guide to creating your own (guitar) chord book. Very user-friendly while presenting a ton of information.

The Advancing Guitarist

By Mick Goodrick

A grab-bag of indispensable thoughts, observations, and studies about the matrix of the guitar. If I had to choose only one book about music to read for the rest of my life, this would be it.

The Music Lesson

By Victor Wooten

A fictionalized story about a guy learning the ropes of Music herself. Very inspiring from a spiritual standpoint. No method or notes to learn here. Just a look into the musician's mind.

The Guitarist's Guide to Composing and Improvising

By Jon Damien

A single-note melody version of *The Chord Factory* with a great section on note clusters and idea "seeds." Lots of ideas for breaking up the routine.

GLOSSARY

Barre - When you use one finger to play multiple strings on the same fret.

Chord diagram - A grid that represents the strings and frets of the 'ukulele on paper. Dots are added to show finger placement.

Chord type - The name given to a group of chords that are created with the same formula.

Closed - A chord in which all the notes fit within one octave.

Enharmonic notes - The five notes named with either a sharp or flat (# or b): A#/Bb, C#/Db, D#/Eb, F#/Gb, and G#/Ab.

Fingerboard - The physical fretboard of an 'ukulele, but also the layout of notes on it.

Formula - A group of numbers that tells you which scale tones to use for a chord.

Inversion - A specific order of notes in a chord shape.
  • **Root inversion** - When the root is the lowest note in the shape.
  • **1st inversion** - When the **3** is the lowest note in the shape.
  • **2nd inversion** - When the **5** is the lowest note in the shape.

Major 3rd or **Minor 3rd** - The interval that gives a chord either a major or minor quality. One is three frets up, one four.

Natural notes - The seven notes without sharp (#) or flat (b) signs - C, D, E, F, G, A, and B.

Open - A chord in which the notes span more than an octave.

Root - The home and first note of a key or chord. What they are named after.

Scale - A sequence of notes that fit the sound of a key.

Scale degree - A specific note in a scale as related to the root, often shown in numbers.

Selective omitting - Reducing more than five-note chords to fit on the 'ukulele's four strings.

Shape - A specific grouping of notes on the fingerboard that creates a chord.

Slash chord - A piano-friendly way of notating hard chords with familiar shapes. Not so nice on the uke.

Substitution - A fancier chord that can replace a "standard" one without changing the tonality of the music.

Triad - A chord made with three notes.

Tritone - A #4 interval that occurs in every dominant chord shape. It has a nasty sound which led people to call it the "Devil's Interval."

Voicing - Same as **Inversion**

ABOUT THE AUTHOR

Brad Bordessa is a graduate of the University of Hawai'i's Institute of Hawaiian Music where he studied music, language, and songwriting. Based on the Hāmākua Coast of Hawai'i Island, Brad performs locally and teaches 'ukulele lessons at various venues. He's a staff instructor for the annual Kahumoku 'Ohana Music and Lifestyle Workshop; the Hawai'i Island 'Ukulele Retreat; and George Kahumoku, Jr.'s Slack Key and 'Ukulele Workshop on Maui.

In addition to teaching classes and workshops, Brad launched LiveUkulele.com in 2006, and it's grown to become one of the top 'ukulele resources on the web. Providing free information to the online 'ukulele community, the site features tabs, industry news, and lessons.

Studying with artists such as Herb Ohta, Jr., James Hill, and George Kahumoku, Jr. has inspired and informed Brad's musical journey, and in 2014 he released his first solo project, *Point A*. This completely self-produced and recorded EP album features five original instrumental pieces. He is currently working on a full-length album.

Search for Brad's music on iTunes or Amazon

Follow Brad's musical journey at BradBordessa.com and on Facebook via @BradBordessa

Find more resources at LiveUkulele.com

Made in the USA
Columbia, SC
23 February 2018